KU-451-301

competent crew

Written by Penny Haire and Sarah Hopkinson
Illustrations by Sarah Selman
Reprinted May 2010
Reprinted April 2011
Reprinted April 2012

www.rya.org.uk

Royal Yachting Association
RYA House, Ensign Way, Hamble, Southampton SO31 4YA
Tel: 0844 556 9555 Fax: 0844 556 9516
email: training@rya.org.uk website: www.rya.org.uk

All rights reserved. No part of this publication may be reproduced, stored in a retrieval
system, or transmitted, in any form or by any means, electronic, mechanical,
photocopying, recording or otherwise, without the prior permission of the publisher.

© Royal Yachting Association 2002

Layout: Batt Creative
Printed in China through World Print

CONTENTS

Sailing is the most exhilarating sport but you need to know the ropes. For the beginner, the best way to learn how to crew a yacht is to take an RYA Competent Crew Course. This book is the ideal companion to the course and you will find it a great help during your first few days afloat.

When I started sailing I lived and instructed at an RYA sea school in the North East. I worked my way up through the RYA Yachtmaster Scheme, first becoming a RYA Yachtmaster then a Yachtmaster Instructor. The skills I learned have been invaluable in my racing career and have been a major part of my success.

Enjoy your course and good sailing.

Dame Ellen MacArthur

O ver 12,000 people, most with absolutely no sailing experience, successfully complete a RYA Competent Crew course every year.

The courses are run by over 220 RYA Training Centres around the UK and overseas. Using a RYA recognised centre will ensure that you are taught to the RYA's high standards, and your course will be safe, informative and enjoyable.

This book *Competent Crew* has been written using the cumulative experience of hundreds of experienced sailing instructors. The techniques shown/described are tried and tested and are suitable for most types of cruising yacht. I hope that you enjoy the book and find it useful. Good sailing!

Craig Burton
Chief Instructor, Sail Cruising

Patrick Roach

It's worth learning the nautical terms because they are exact definitions of technical features, so no confusion, and they will help you understand the sport and learn more quickly. The nautical terms are used throughout this book.

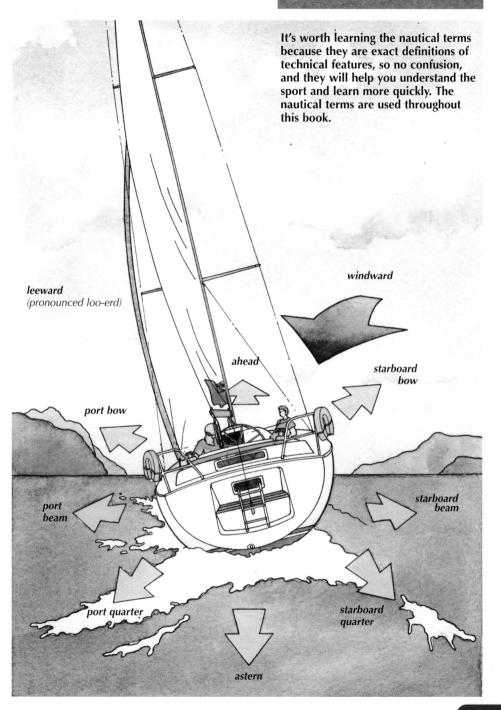

leeward
(pronounced loo-erd)

windward

ahead

starboard bow

port bow

port beam

starboard beam

port quarter

starboard quarter

astern

Cruiser racer

These boats mix good performance with comfort. When racing, heavy items can be removed from the boat. Many owners will have two sets of sails – one for cruising and one for racing.

Sailing boats come in all shapes and sizes, and can be very specialised. Designers attempt to strike the right balance between comfort and performance.

Traditional craft

Many people enjoy sailing on this type of vessel. Used in the past for coastal trade.

Motor sailer

These boats are a compromise between sailing performance and comfort, with a powerful engine to get you there in adverse winds.

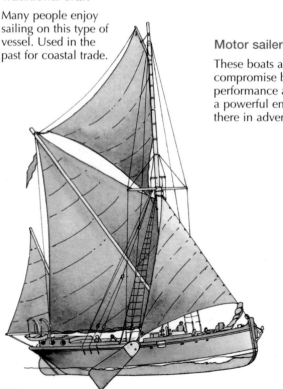

Small cruiser with junk rig and bilge keels

Rig style from the Far East. Easily controlled by one person.

Small racing yacht or keelboat

Designed for day racing, mostly inshore. These boats are light, high performance, demanding and exciting to sail.

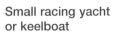

Medium or large cruising yacht

Comfort, ease of handling, reliability and safety are usually the main features of this type of boat.

Cruising catamaran

Multihulls can provide a combination of good performance and comfort. Many have undertaken long ocean passages.

Cruising yacht with windsurfer rig

This type of rig is easy to handle when short-handed.

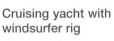

Racing trimaran (3 hulls) or catamaran (2 hulls)

This is about as fast as you'll get to go on a sailing boat. Fast, exciting, unforgiving – for experienced sailors only!

Square rigger

Restored or newly built boats are used for sail training and 'Tall Ships' events.

Long keel classic craft

A long keel and well-balanced sails make these boats hold a very straight and steady course at sea – but under power in a marina they can be hard to manoeuvre.

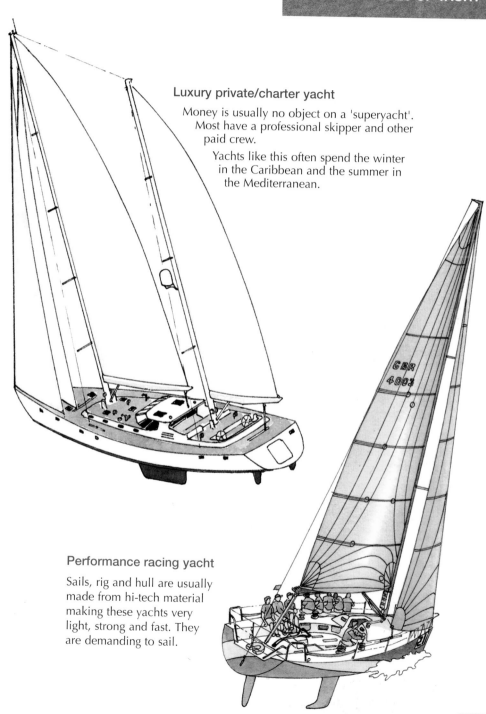

Luxury private/charter yacht

Money is usually no object on a 'superyacht'. Most have a professional skipper and other paid crew.

Yachts like this often spend the winter in the Caribbean and the summer in the Mediterranean.

Performance racing yacht

Sails, rig and hull are usually made from hi-tech material making these yachts very light, strong and fast. They are demanding to sail.

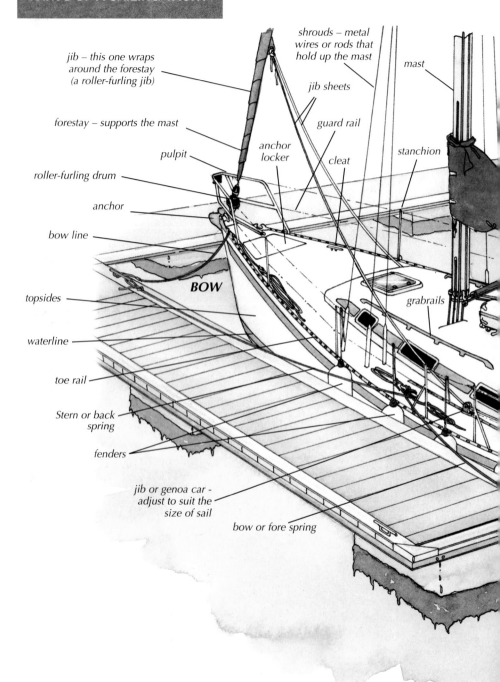

jib – this one wraps around the forestay (a roller-furling jib)

shrouds – metal wires or rods that hold up the mast

mast

jib sheets

forestay – supports the mast

guard rail

pulpit

anchor locker

cleat

stanchion

roller-furling drum

anchor

bow line

topsides

BOW

grabrails

waterline

toe rail

Stern or back spring

fenders

jib or genoa car – adjust to suit the size of sail

bow or fore spring

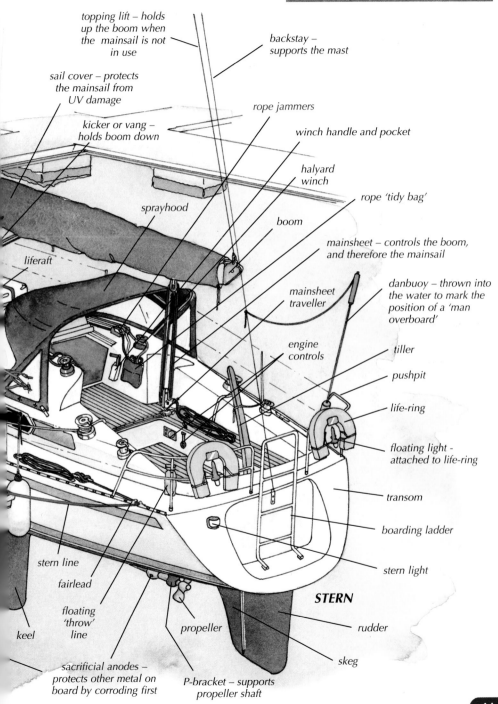

topping lift – holds up the boom when the mainsail is not in use

backstay – supports the mast

sail cover – protects the mainsail from UV damage

rope jammers

kicker or vang – holds boom down

winch handle and pocket

halyard winch

rope 'tidy bag'

sprayhood

boom

mainsheet – controls the boom, and therefore the mainsail

liferaft

mainsheet traveller

danbuoy – thrown into the water to mark the position of a 'man overboard'

engine controls

tiller

pushpit

life-ring

floating light - attached to life-ring

transom

boarding ladder

stern light

STERN

stern line

fairlead

floating 'throw' line

keel

propeller

rudder

skeg

sacrificial anodes – protects other metal on board by corroding first

P-bracket – supports propeller shaft

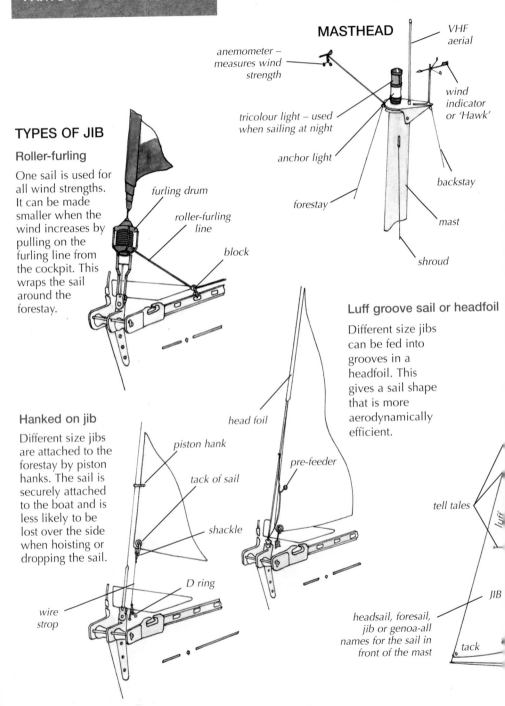

MASTHEAD

VHF aerial

anemometer – measures wind strength

tricolour light – used when sailing at night

anchor light

wind indicator or 'Hawk'

backstay

forestay

mast

shroud

TYPES OF JIB

Roller-furling

One sail is used for all wind strengths. It can be made smaller when the wind increases by pulling on the furling line from the cockpit. This wraps the sail around the forestay.

furling drum

roller-furling line

block

Hanked on jib

Different size jibs are attached to the forestay by piston hanks. The sail is securely attached to the boat and is less likely to be lost over the side when hoisting or dropping the sail.

piston hank

tack of sail

shackle

D ring

wire strop

head foil

pre-feeder

Luff groove sail or headfoil

Different size jibs can be fed into grooves in a headfoil. This gives a sail shape that is more aerodynamically efficient.

tell tales

luff

JIB

headsail, foresail, jib or genoa-all names for the sail in front of the mast

tack

RIGGING AND SAILS

How a reefing pennant is rigged

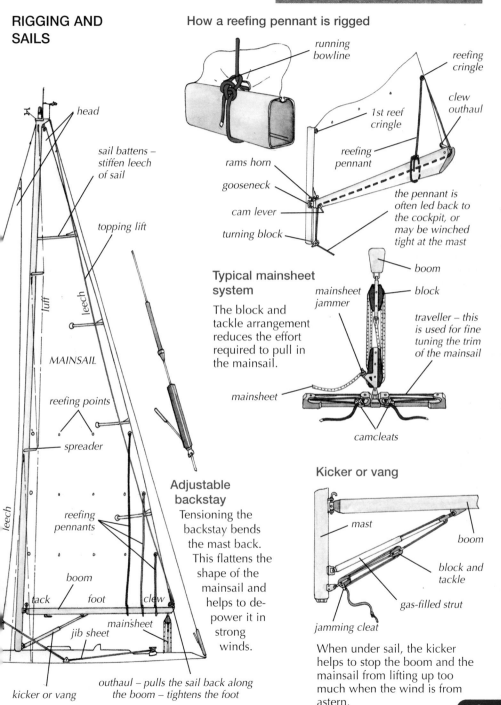

running bowline

reefing cringle

head

sail battens – stiffen leech of sail

clew outhaul

1st reef cringle

rams horn

gooseneck

reefing pennant

cam lever

turning block

the pennant is often led back to the cockpit, or may be winched tight at the mast

topping lift

luff

leech

MAINSAIL

boom

block

Typical mainsheet system

mainsheet jammer

traveller – this is used for fine tuning the trim of the mainsail

The block and tackle arrangement reduces the effort required to pull in the mainsail.

reefing points

mainsheet

spreader

camcleats

Kicker or vang

Adjustable backstay

reefing pennants

Tensioning the backstay bends the mast back. This flattens the shape of the mainsail and helps to de-power it in strong winds.

mast

boom

leech

block and tackle

gas-filled strut

boom

jamming cleat

tack   foot   clew

jib sheet

mainsheet

kicker or vang

outhaul – pulls the sail back along the boom – tightens the foot

When under sail, the kicker helps to stop the boom and the mainsail from lifting up too much when the wind is from astern.

13

Figure-of-eight

Used as a stopper knot to prevent a rope running through a car or jammer.

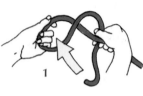

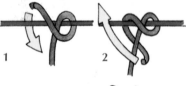

Clove hitch

For tying on fenders or other uses such as lashing the tiller amidships.

Rolling hitch

Used for temporarily relieving the strain on a working rope, eg, if you have a riding turn (jam) on a winch.

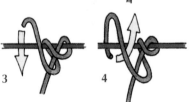

Slides this way

Will take the weight off this rope.

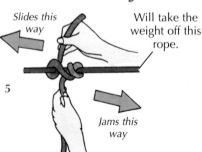

Jams this way

Bowline

Makes a loop in the end of a rope. Used to attach the jib sheets or to make a loop for mooring.

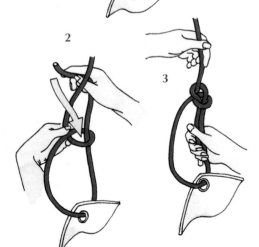

KNOTS

Round turn and two half-hitches

A versatile knot with many uses such as securing a mooring line to a ring or hanging a fender.

1

2

3

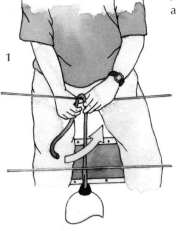

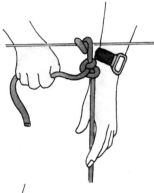

Single sheet bend

Used to join two ropes – useful to lengthen a mooring line. For ropes of different thicknesses, the yellow rope would be the thicker one.

1

2

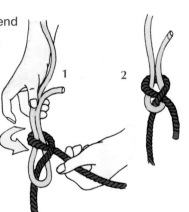

Double sheet bend

More secure and is also used to tie a smaller line to a larger one.

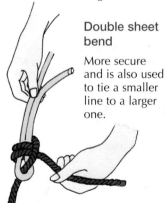

Reef knot

Useful to tie in reefs to tidy the sail – but not secure enough for mooring lines.

1

2

3

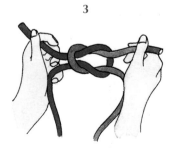

  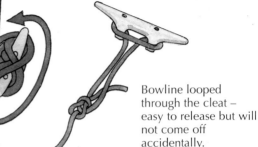

Making fast to a cleat

Take the rope round the cleat, add one or more figure-of-eights and make another round turn to secure. OXO is a good way to remember this.

Bowline looped through the cleat – easy to release but will not come off accidentally.

Bowlines dipped through and onto the bollard – easy for any vessel to leave.

Bowline on a ring – the round turn reduces chafe.

Coiling a rope

1 Pulling your arms apart the same amount for each coil will help you make even size loops.

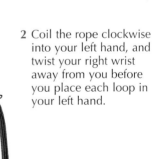

2 Coil the rope clockwise into your left hand, and twist your right wrist away from you before you place each loop in your left hand.

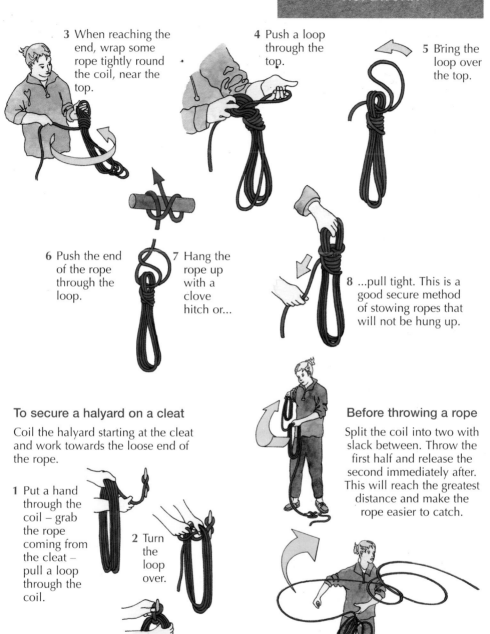

3 When reaching the end, wrap some rope tightly round the coil, near the top.

4 Push a loop through the top.

5 Bring the loop over the top.

6 Push the end of the rope through the loop.

7 Hang the rope up with a clove hitch or...

8 ...pull tight. This is a good secure method of stowing ropes that will not be hung up.

To secure a halyard on a cleat

Coil the halyard starting at the cleat and work towards the loose end of the rope.

1 Put a hand through the coil – grab the rope coming from the cleat – pull a loop through the coil.

2 Turn the loop over.

3 Push the loop over the cleat and pull the coil downwards.

Before throwing a rope

Split the coil into two with slack between. Throw the first half and release the second immediately after. This will reach the greatest distance and make the rope easier to catch.

Sweating up a halyard

1 Pull out with the right hand while keeping the rope secure on the cleat with the left hand.

2 Take up the slack with the left hand as you pull down with the right.

Do not wrap the rope round your hand.

Using a block with a cam cleat

Pull the rope up to jam it – pull through the jammer to tighten.

Pull the rope down to release from jammer. You can then ease the rope out.

Keep your fingers well away from the jammer.

Using rope jammers

A rope can be tightened by pulling or winching through a closed jamming cleat.

Do not release under load - keep fingers away.

To release a rope in a jammer

Winch in the rope a little first, then hold the tension on the winch and fully open the jammer.

Using winches

1 Load the
rope round
the winch
clockwise.

3 Keep the tension on while using the
winch handle. Many winches have
two gears.

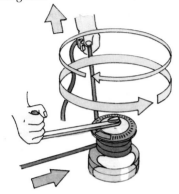

2 Keep the tension on
and put two turns
round the winch. Have
your little finger nearest
the winch and keep
sliding the hand away
from the winch.

A self-tailing winch
holds the rope in a
groove at the top.

Use a flat hand to
ease the rope out.

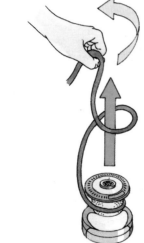

For a fast release – spin the
rope vertically upwards to
clear the turns off the
winch and then let go!
Make sure the sheet will
run out smoothly.

Crew working together –
to provide tension on the
sheet – watch the sail and
wind the winch.

Never wrap rope round your hand when holding it, pulling on it…or using a winch.
Keep hands and fingers away from winches and jammers.

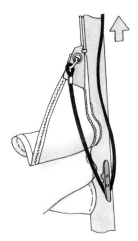

Most skippers motor out of the marina and harbour but will always have the sails ready for use.

- The engine may stop unexpectedly
- It's easier to get everything ready in the shelter of harbour

Main

1 Take off the mainsail cover. Fold and stow it.

2 Attach the main halyard making sure it is led from the masthead to the head of the sail correctly – not around the rigging.

3 Loop the halyard round a cleat and pull tight so the sail is ready to go up but is secure. (Don't do this with a wire halyard as it may damage the halyard, the cleat and the mast.)

stopper knot

4 Undo the coils of the mainsheet but keep it jammed tight until the crew have finished working around the boom.

5 Take care when working on the coach roof. Close the main hatch to avoid falling down the companionway.

Jib

- Attach the tack of the sail to the D ring and hank the sail to the forestay
- Clip the halyard to the head of the sail and to the pulpit
- Tie the sheets to the clew of the sail and lead them back to the cockpit correctly
- Add a figure-of-eight knot to the end of the sheets
- Move the sheet cars on both side decks to the correct position
- Secure the sail neatly to the top guard rail

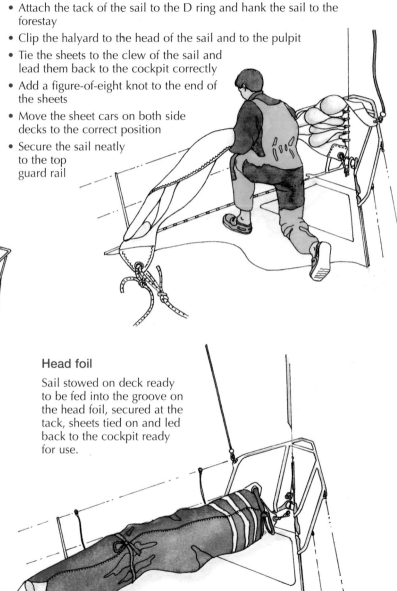

Head foil

Sail stowed on deck ready to be fed into the groove on the head foil, secured at the tack, sheets tied on and led back to the cockpit ready for use.

1 Remove the sail ties.

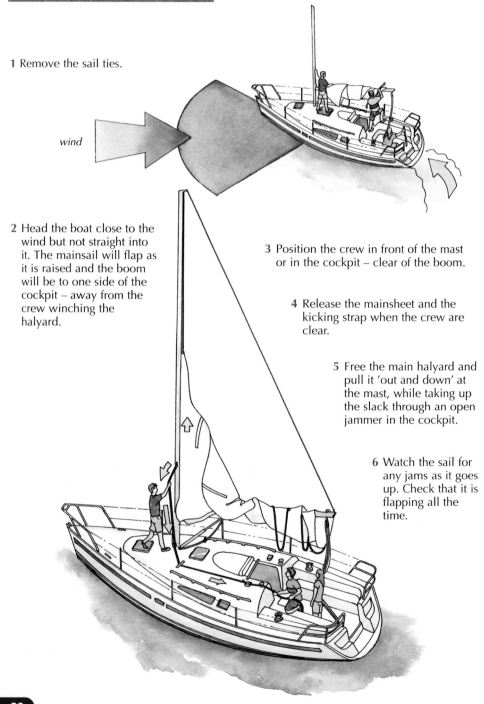

wind

2 Head the boat close to the wind but not straight into it. The mainsail will flap as it is raised and the boom will be to one side of the cockpit – away from the crew winching the halyard.

3 Position the crew in front of the mast or in the cockpit – clear of the boom.

4 Release the mainsheet and the kicking strap when the crew are clear.

5 Free the main halyard and pull it 'out and down' at the mast, while taking up the slack through an open jammer in the cockpit.

6 Watch the sail for any jams as it goes up. Check that it is flapping all the time.

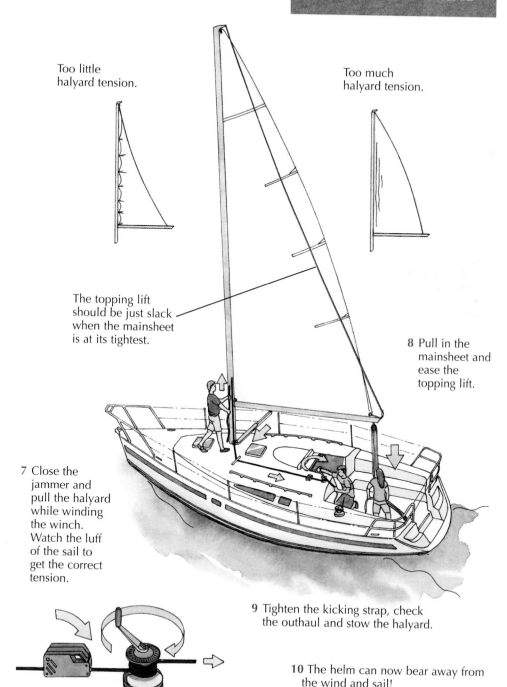

Too little
halyard tension.

Too much
halyard tension.

The topping lift
should be just slack
when the mainsheet
is at its tightest.

8 Pull in the
mainsheet and
ease the
topping lift.

7 Close the
jammer and
pull the halyard
while winding
the winch.
Watch the luff
of the sail to
get the correct
tension.

9 Tighten the kicking strap, check
the outhaul and stow the halyard.

10 The helm can now bear away from
the wind and sail!

A roller-furling jib

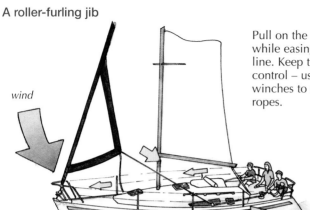

wind

Pull on the leeward sheet while easing out the furling line. Keep the sail under control – use cleats and winches to control the ropes.

Not all of the sail needs to be unfurled every time. In windy conditions keep the jib smaller.

With a small sail, move the genoa car forward to put equal tension on the leech and foot.

A hanked-on foresail

1 Make the sail ready to go – remove ties and release the halyard.

2 Release the sheet.

3 Pull the halyard 'out and down' at the mast while taking up the slack through an open jammer in the cockpit.

4 Watch the sail does not snag as it goes up.

5 Close the jammer, pull the halyard while winding the winch. Watch the luff of the sail to get the correct tension.

wind

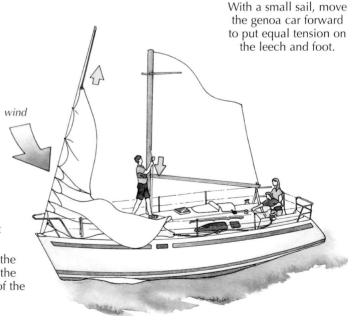

6 Pull in and winch tight the sheet on the leeward side to the correct tension – and sail!

A loose-luffed jib

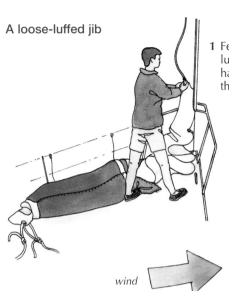

1 Feed the head into the luff groove, attach the halyard and release the ties.

wind

2 Feed the luff of the sail into the groove while the halyard is slowly pulled to raise the sail. Watch for snags as it goes up and make sure it stays in the pre-feeder.

Set the halyard tension then pull in the sheets – jib then main – no more than is necessary to stop them flapping.

Too little halyard tension.

Too much halyard tension.

TOO MUCH SAIL ON A WINDY DAY

- Makes the boat difficult to steer straight – the wheel or tiller is too heavy
- Causes the boat to heel (lean over) excessively

Three reefs give a main that will reef up to 60% of its total area.

Trisail

A very small strong sail rigged instead of the main in very strong winds.

Sheets

Loose foot

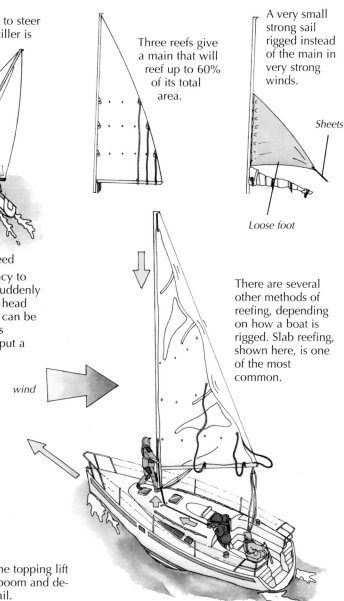

- Makes the boat lose speed
- Gives the boat a tendency to broach in gusts – heel suddenly and uncontrollably and head towards the wind – this can be alarming and sometimes dangerous - it's time to put a reef in

Reefing

wind

1 Send the crew to the mast wearing a harness.
2 Head the boat close to, but not straight into the wind.
3 Ease out the kicking strap then the mainsheet.

There are several other methods of reefing, depending on how a boat is rigged. Slab reefing, shown here, is one of the most common.

4 Pull up on the topping lift to raise the boom and de-power the sail.

5 With the mainsail flapping, lift the jammer and ease the halyard. Pull the sail down and hook the cringle in the luff of the sail over the rams horn and hold it in position.

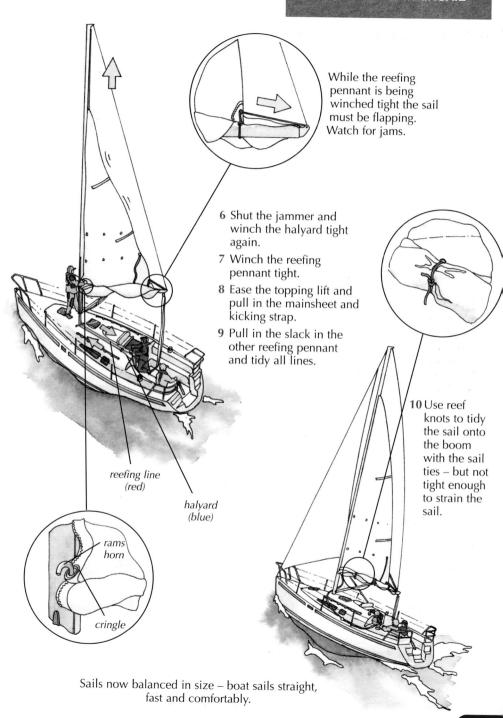

While the reefing pennant is being winched tight the sail must be flapping. Watch for jams.

6 Shut the jammer and winch the halyard tight again.

7 Winch the reefing pennant tight.

8 Ease the topping lift and pull in the mainsheet and kicking strap.

9 Pull in the slack in the other reefing pennant and tidy all lines.

10 Use reef knots to tidy the sail onto the boom with the sail ties – but not tight enough to strain the sail.

reefing line
(red)

halyard
(blue)

rams
horn

cringle

Sails now balanced in size – boat sails straight, fast and comfortably.

Roller-furling jib

Pull on the furling line to rotate the forestay and furl the jib. Ease out the sheet, keeping it under tension to ensure a smooth furl.

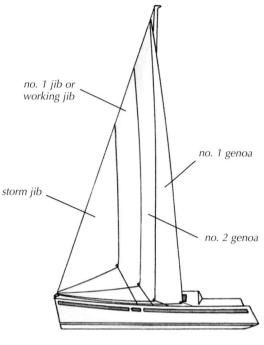

no. 1 jib or working jib

no. 1 genoa

storm jib

no. 2 genoa

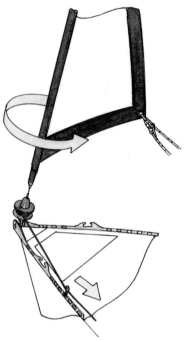

When you change the size of the headsail you will need to change the position of the car as well.

Hanked-on jib

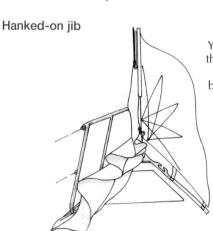

You can prepare the new headsail for hoisting before you drop the old one.

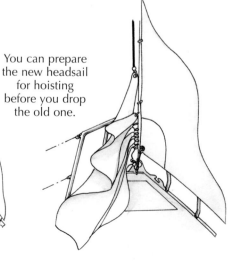

Dropping the headsail

1 Ease out the halyard.

2 Pull down on the luff of the sail – keep some tension on the jib sheet – so neither the sail nor the sheet go over the side.

Large headsails may need two people on the foredeck to control the sail.

3 Remove the halyard from the sail and clip it onto the pulpit – re-tension the halyard.

4 Pull the sail back and roll it so it can be tied to the guard rail to use again.

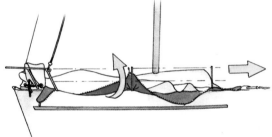

5 Or if not required again, fold it from the clew forward. Remove the hanks and stuff it into its sailbag.

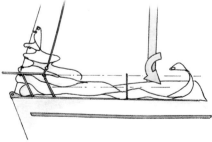

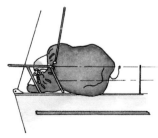

6 Keep the bag and sail tied in place!

7 Coil up and tidy away all sheets and the halyard.

STOWING THE MAINSAIL

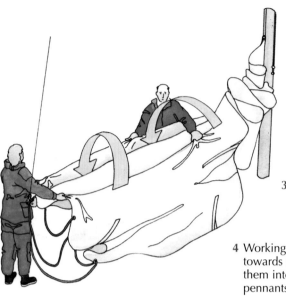

Bagging the mainsail

1 Check the mainsheet and topping lift are tensioned and secure. Close the main hatch before working beside the boom.

2 Push all the sail to one side of the boom – the leeward side is easiest.

3 With crew at either end of the boom, make a bag of sail on the windward side of the boom.

4 Working together, grab folds of sail – pull towards the back of the boom and push them into the bag. Lift in the slack reefing pennants too.

5 Keep working until all the sail is in the bag – roll the bag tight and lift it onto the top of the boom. Secure with sail ties.

Flaking the mainsail

1 Push all the sail to one side of the boom - leeward side is easier.

2 With crew at either end of the boom, flake the sail from one side of the boom to the other in even-sized folds – keep pulling the sail towards the stern to keep it flat.

3 Hold the sail in place with the sail ties – secure the head of the sail.

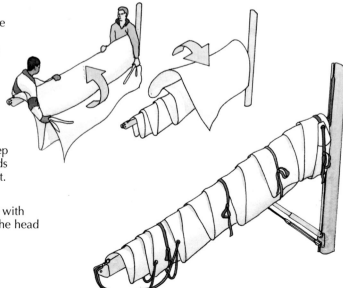

Flaking and bagging the jib

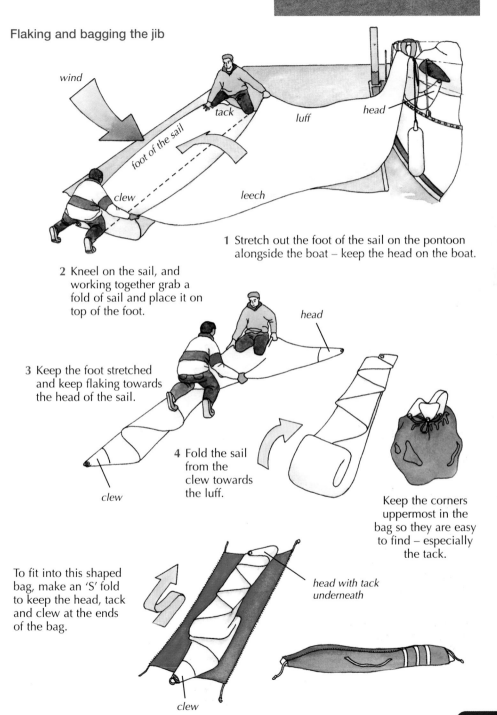

wind

tack   luff   head

foot of the sail

clew   leech

1 Stretch out the foot of the sail on the pontoon alongside the boat – keep the head on the boat.

2 Kneel on the sail, and working together grab a fold of sail and place it on top of the foot.

head

3 Keep the foot stretched and keep flaking towards the head of the sail.

4 Fold the sail from the clew towards the luff.

clew

Keep the corners uppermost in the bag so they are easy to find – especially the tack.

To fit into this shaped bag, make an 'S' fold to keep the head, tack and clew at the ends of the bag.

head with tack underneath

clew

When you put a spoon into running water it is sucked into the flow.

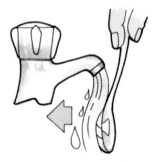

The flow of air over the sail produces pressure changes, producing lift and increasing the speed of the wind blowing over the upper surface – like an aircraft's wing.

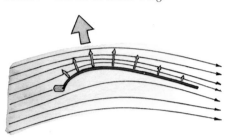

A combination of a sideways force from the sail and opposite resistance from the water pushes the boat forward like squeezing a bar of wet soap.

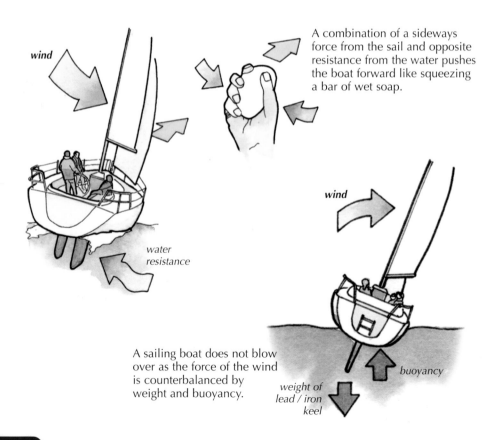

wind

water resistance

wind

A sailing boat does not blow over as the force of the wind is counterbalanced by weight and buoyancy.

weight of lead / iron keel

buoyancy

A modern yacht will sail at any angle to the wind apart from the 'no-go' zone – an angle of about 45° each side of the wind direction.

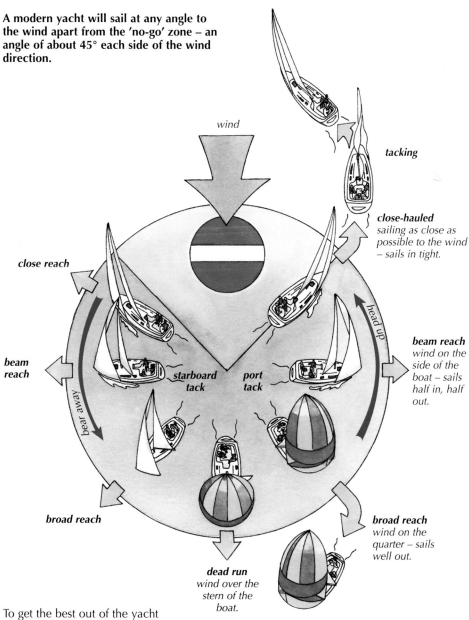

wind

tacking

close-hauled
sailing as close as possible to the wind – sails in tight.

close reach

head up

beam reach
wind on the side of the boat – sails half in, half out.

beam reach

starboard tack

port tack

bear away

broad reach

broad reach
wind on the quarter – sails well out.

dead run
wind over the stern of the boat.

To get the best out of the yacht the sails must be correctly trimmed for each point of sailing. A change in course inevitably means the sails must be re-trimmed.

Close-hauled - correct course

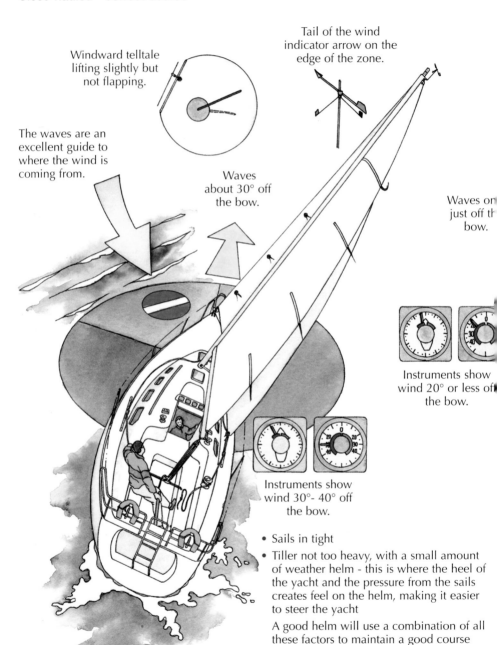

Tail of the wind indicator arrow on the edge of the zone.

Windward telltale lifting slightly but not flapping.

The waves are an excellent guide to where the wind is coming from.

Waves about 30° off the bow.

Waves on just off th bow.

Instruments show wind 20° or less of the bow.

Instruments show wind 30°- 40° off the bow.

- Sails in tight
- Tiller not too heavy, with a small amount of weather helm - this is where the heel of the yacht and the pressure from the sails creates feel on the helm, making it easier to steer the yacht

A good helm will use a combination of all these factors to maintain a good course and keep the yacht 'in the groove'

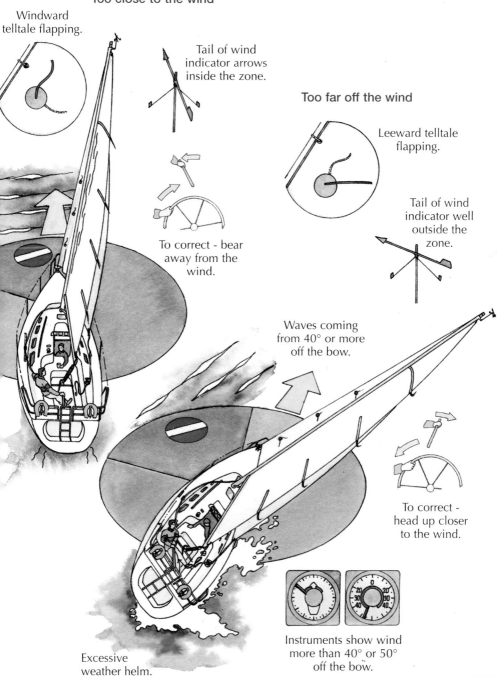

Too close to the wind

Windward telltale flapping.

Tail of wind indicator arrows inside the zone.

Too far off the wind

Leeward telltale flapping.

Tail of wind indicator well outside the zone.

To correct - bear away from the wind.

Waves coming from 40° or more off the bow.

To correct - head up closer to the wind.

Excessive weather helm.

Instruments show wind more than 40° or 50° off the bow.

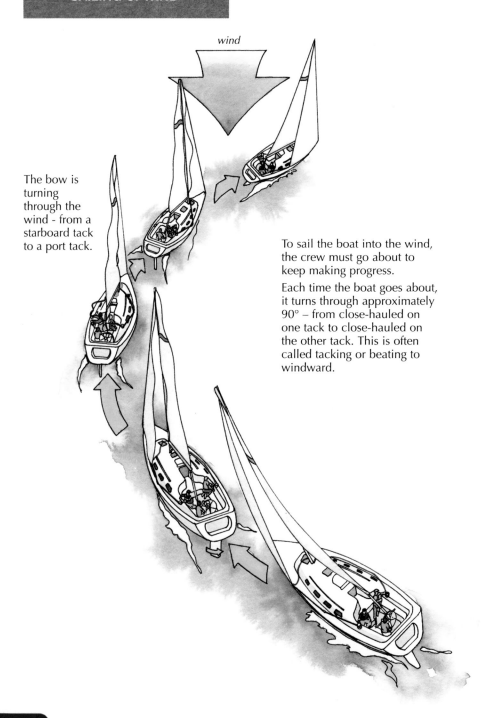

wind

The bow is turning through the wind - from a starboard tack to a port tack.

To sail the boat into the wind, the crew must go about to keep making progress.

Each time the boat goes about, it turns through approximately 90° – from close-hauled on one tack to close-hauled on the other tack. This is often called tacking or beating to windward.

Turning the boat's bow through the wind – from close-hauled on one tack to close-hauled on the other. Remember to look around before changing course.

Look around. Helmsman calls "Ready about". Crew prepares the jib sheets.

When all ready helmsman calls "helm to lee" and turns the bow towards the wind.

Head to wind – the crew lets fly the old jib sheet making sure it can run free, and quickly pulls in the new one, ready to winch in.

The sails have changed sides on to a port tack and begin to fill. Centre the helm.

Crew fine tunes the sail trim and tidies up.

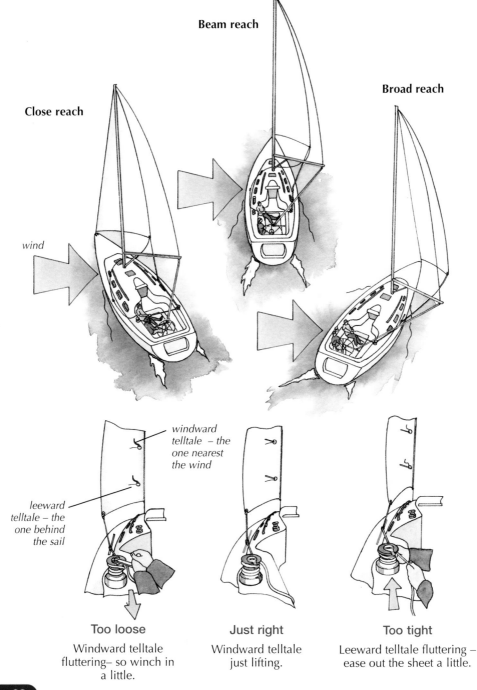

Beam reach

Broad reach

Close reach

wind

windward telltale – the one nearest the wind

leeward telltale – the one behind the sail

Too loose

Windward telltale fluttering– so winch in a little.

Just right

Windward telltale just lifting.

Too tight

Leeward telltale fluttering – ease out the sheet a little.

Sailing with the wind abaft or behind the beam of the boat.

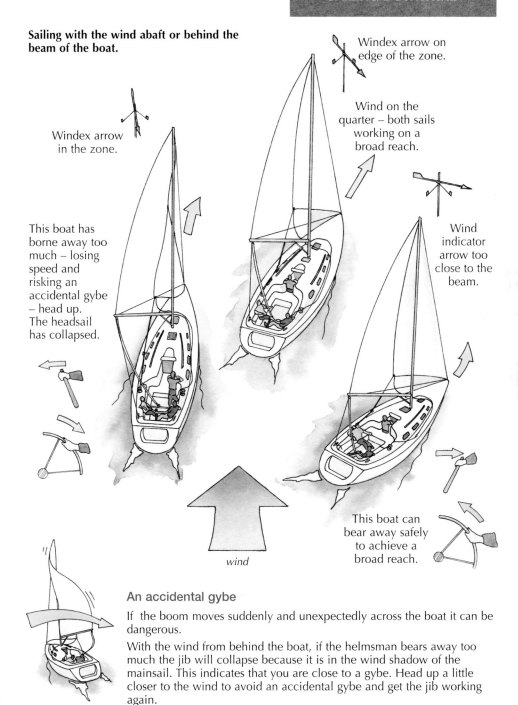

Windex arrow on edge of the zone.

Wind on the quarter – both sails working on a broad reach.

Windex arrow in the zone.

This boat has borne away too much – losing speed and risking an accidental gybe – head up. The headsail has collapsed.

Wind indicator arrow too close to the beam.

This boat can bear away safely to achieve a broad reach.

wind

An accidental gybe

If the boom moves suddenly and unexpectedly across the boat it can be dangerous.

With the wind from behind the boat, if the helmsman bears away too much the jib will collapse because it is in the wind shadow of the mainsail. This indicates that you are close to a gybe. Head up a little closer to the wind to avoid an accidental gybe and get the jib working again.

Poled-out headsail

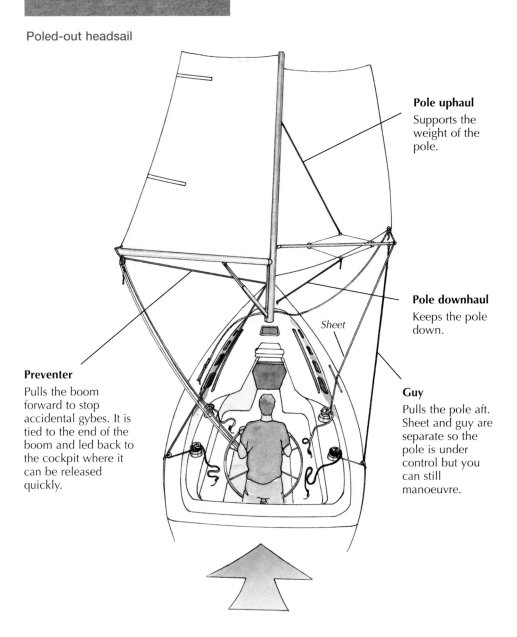

Pole uphaul
Supports the weight of the pole.

Pole downhaul
Keeps the pole down.

Sheet

Preventer
Pulls the boom forward to stop accidental gybes. It is tied to the end of the boom and led back to the cockpit where it can be released quickly.

Guy
Pulls the pole aft. Sheet and guy are separate so the pole is under control but you can still manoeuvre.

Wind Dead Astern
(The mainsail is on the port side so the boat is on STARBOARD tack)

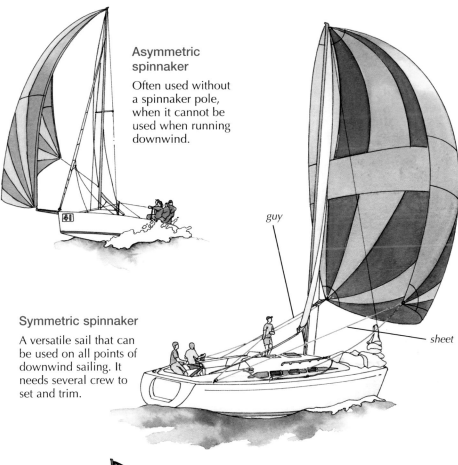

Asymmetric spinnaker

Often used without a spinnaker pole, when it cannot be used when running downwind.

guy

sheet

Symmetric spinnaker

A versatile sail that can be used on all points of downwind sailing. It needs several crew to set and trim.

Cruising chute

Made from similar material to a spinnaker but rigged like a genoa. It is set without a pole, uphaul, downhaul or guy; this makes it easy to handle. It does not set very well when running downwind.

When sailing downwind it is often faster overall and safer to zig zag downwind, sailing a series of broad reaches using a controlled gybe.

Wind changes to port quarter and the boat gybes - mainsail and jib change sides.

wind

A controlled gybe from a broad reach or a run is a safe procedure.

The helmsman starts the sequence by calling 'stand by to gybe'. If a gybe preventer is rigged it is released. The crew sheets the mainsail in and prepares the headsail sheets.

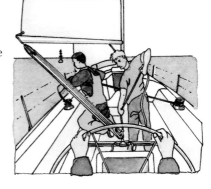

When the main is in the middle the helmsman turns the wheel to gybe.

The main flips across, sheet the jib in on the same side as the main and when it is under tension release the other sheet.

The mainsheet is eased out.

The crew make final adjustments to sail trim. The gybe preventer may be rigged again.

When a yacht is turned it will pivot about the keel. The rudder is moved by pushing or pulling on the tiller or turning the wheel.

Tiller steering

Push the tiller to port to turn the boat to starboard and vice versa.

Wheel steering

Turn the wheel the same way you want to turn the boat.

If you are off course, correcting takes practice. Make a small alteration, straighten up and check the effect on the compass. Average the course - if you have consistently sailed on one side of the course, compensate by sailing an equal amount on the other.

Too far to port	Correct course	Too far to starboard

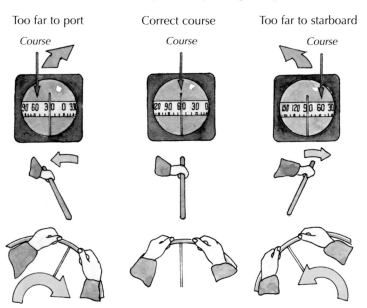

To steer a straight and steady course at sea, check the compass from time to time and watch the bow of the boat relative to the horizon.

Use as many references as you can to orientate yourself; for example, the position of the sun, angle of the waves and the wind.

One of the best references is an object in front of you; you can even use a cloud for a short while. An occasional check on the compass should keep you on a steady course.

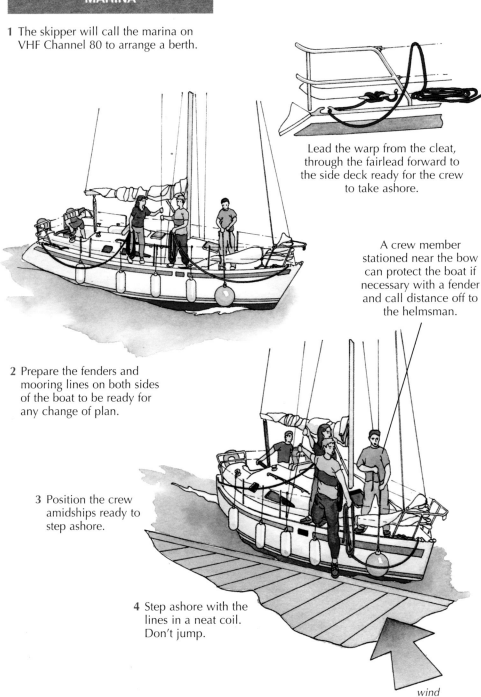

1 The skipper will call the marina on VHF Channel 80 to arrange a berth.

Lead the warp from the cleat, through the fairlead forward to the side deck ready for the crew to take ashore.

A crew member stationed near the bow can protect the boat if necessary with a fender and call distance off to the helmsman.

2 Prepare the fenders and mooring lines on both sides of the boat to be ready for any change of plan.

3 Position the crew amidships ready to step ashore.

4 Step ashore with the lines in a neat coil. Don't jump.

wind

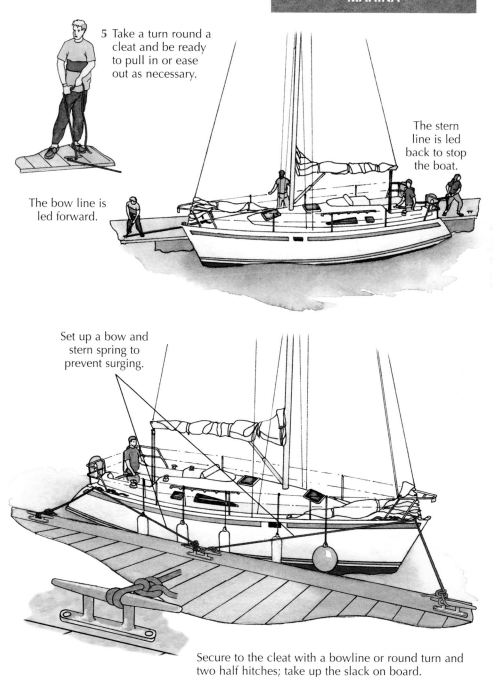

5 Take a turn round a cleat and be ready to pull in or ease out as necessary.

The stern line is led back to stop the boat.

The bow line is led forward.

Set up a bow and stern spring to prevent surging.

Secure to the cleat with a bowline or round turn and two half hitches; take up the slack on board.

1 If possible, first ask the other boat if they are about to leave.

2 Moor to the other vessel using fenders rigged higher than normal, bow line, stern line and springs. Then lead long lines ashore so that all the weight of your boat is not hanging on the other boat's lines. Check the boats are parallel – so you don't end up bows in.

3 Make sure the lines are long enough to allow for any rise and fall of tide.

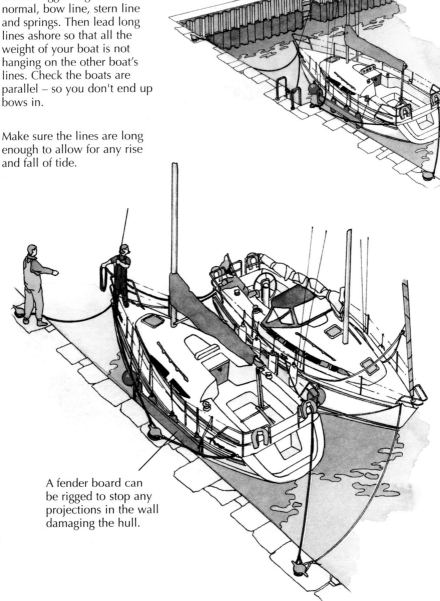

A fender board can be rigged to stop any projections in the wall damaging the hull.

Alongside berth

Get the lines ready to slip; remember the short end of the line should be on top of the cleat.

Motoring ahead on a bow spring forces the bow in and the stern out.

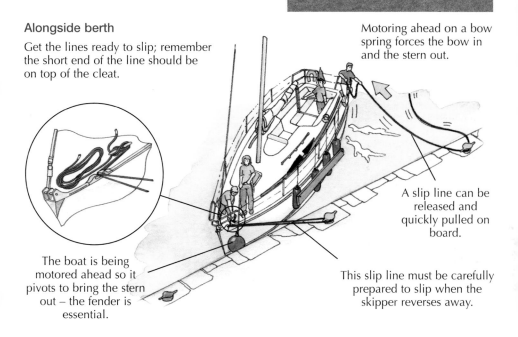

A slip line can be released and quickly pulled on board.

The boat is being motored ahead so it pivots to bring the stern out – the fender is essential.

This slip line must be carefully prepared to slip when the skipper reverses away.

Leaving a raft

Crew ready to pull in bow line from the boat to the shore.

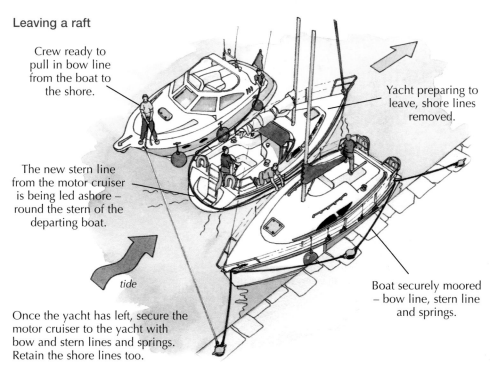

Yacht preparing to leave, shore lines removed.

The new stern line from the motor cruiser is being led ashore – round the stern of the departing boat.

tide

Boat securely moored – bow line, stern line and springs.

Once the yacht has left, secure the motor cruiser to the yacht with bow and stern lines and springs. Retain the shore lines too.

1 The skipper will approach the mooring in the same direction as the other moored yachts are lying – usually into the tidal stream or head to wind if no tide.

2 Point towards the buoy and call the distances – the helmsman probably can't see the buoy.

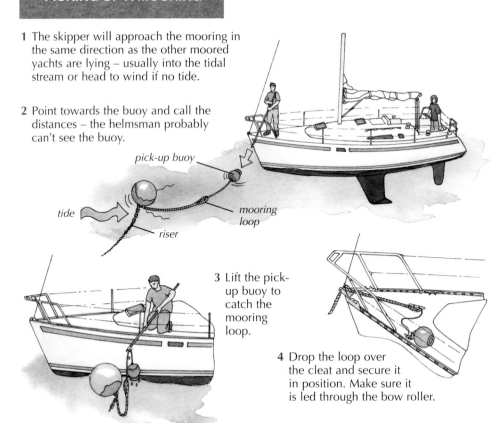

pick-up buoy

tide

mooring loop

riser

3 Lift the pick-up buoy to catch the mooring loop.

4 Drop the loop over the cleat and secure it in position. Make sure it is led through the bow roller.

Where there is no pick-up buoy or rope

Be ready to lean down to the buoy.

1 One crew catches the buoy by the ring whilst the other attaches a mooring warp.

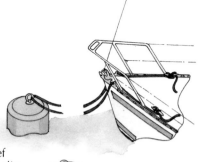

2 For a brief stay rig a slip line through the ring on the buoy using a mooring warp.

The buoy may be very heavy.

3 For an overnight stop secure with a round turn and a bowline.

Dropping anchor

Secure to the cleat; make sure that the end of the chain that goes back into the locker is on top of the cleat.

If necessary secure a tripping line to the anchor and lead it so it cannot get caught up when the anchor is put down.

Bruce anchor

bow roller

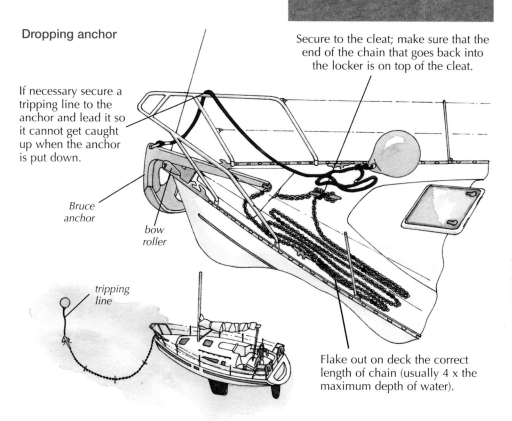

tripping line

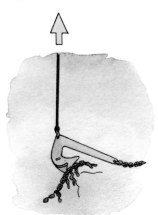

Flake out on deck the correct length of chain (usually 4 x the maximum depth of water).

Weighing anchor

If the anchor is fouled, use the trip line to pull it free.

Pull up the chain to raise the anchor – bend your knees, not your back.

The skipper will motor the boat gently forward to take the weight off the chain.

SAILING VESSELS

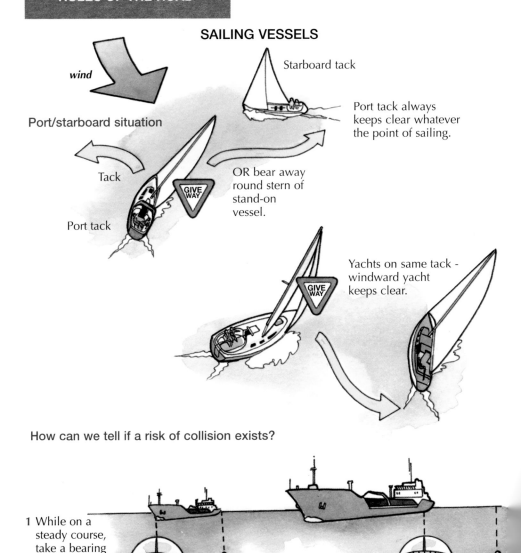

wind

Starboard tack

Port/starboard situation

Port tack always keeps clear whatever the point of sailing.

Tack

OR bear away round stern of stand-on vessel.

GIVE WAY

Port tack

GIVE WAY

Yachts on same tack - windward yacht keeps clear.

How can we tell if a risk of collision exists?

1 While on a steady course, take a bearing of the ship or line it up with a part of your boat such as a stanchion or stay.

2 If the bearing of the ship changes or moves in relation to your stanchion there will not be a collision.

If the bearing stays steady or the ship remains lined up with your stanchion - a risk of collision exists.

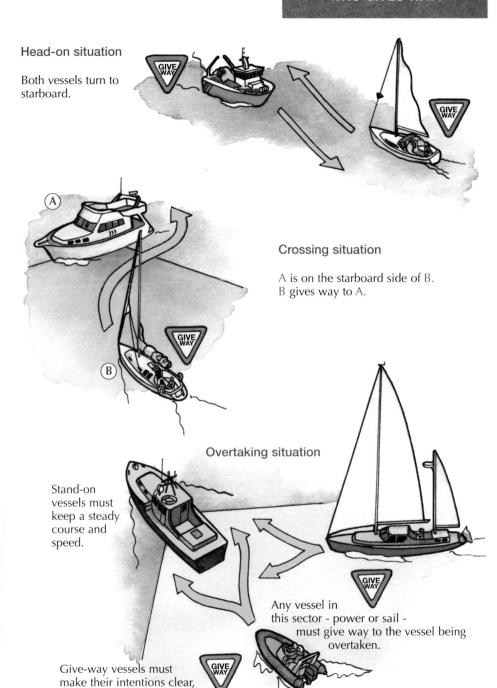

Head-on situation

Both vessels turn to starboard.

Crossing situation

A is on the starboard side of B. B gives way to A.

Overtaking situation

Stand-on vessels must keep a steady course and speed.

Any vessel in this sector - power or sail - must give way to the vessel being overtaken.

Give-way vessels must make their intentions clear, by making an early, bold alteration of course.

GIVE WAY

DAY look out for:

- Racing marks and fishing pots.
- Fast approaching sea-cat and ship.
- Rubbish in the water.
- Yacht on closing course
  - who is the give-way vessel?
- Where is the shipping lane?
  - are we out of the way of the ships?
  - where are the buoys?
  - what is the depth on the echo sounder? Too shallow and we might go aground. Too deep and we could be in the main shipping channel.
- Listen to the VHF for information.

NIGHT look out for:

- Lights
  - flashing lights are navigation marks – buoys, beacons, lighthouses.
  - fixed lights at sea are boats.
  - near harbours it can be difficult to spot vessels or buoys because of the background lights.
- All crew should clip on.
- Watch for unlit buoys and flotsam.
- Do not use lights down below – it ruins everyone's night vision.
- Watch for small boats moving – not just ships.

You will probably keep watches if you are sailing for longer than a normal day.

A good skipper doesn't wait until nightfall to start the rota when everyone is already tired. They will share out duties, make sure the crew keep warm and dry and have suitable meals.

A good watch keeping rota will prevent the crew being alone, tired and cold at night.

When you are on watch make sure you look all around you and behind the jib periodically.

When you are coming on watch arrive in good time.

In harbour, raise the Ensign at 0800 (summer) and 0900 (winter). Lower the Ensign at sunset or 2100 BST, whichever is earlier.

The Ensign is flown day and night at sea.

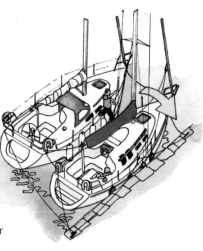

Before mooring alongside ask – then walk round by the foredeck to go ashore – quietly. Don't wake up other crew when you return.

Do not dump rubbish in the sea.

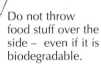

Do not throw food stuff over the side – even if it is biodegradable.

Do not use the heads in the marina unless you have a holding tank.

Do not pump or spill oil, diesel, paint or other chemicals into the water.

Every year more accidents happen to crews going ashore by dinghy than at any other time, so...

Wear lifejackets.

Do not overload the boat – make two trips if necessary.

Carry oars, the dinghy pump and spare fuel for the outboard, just in case.

pump

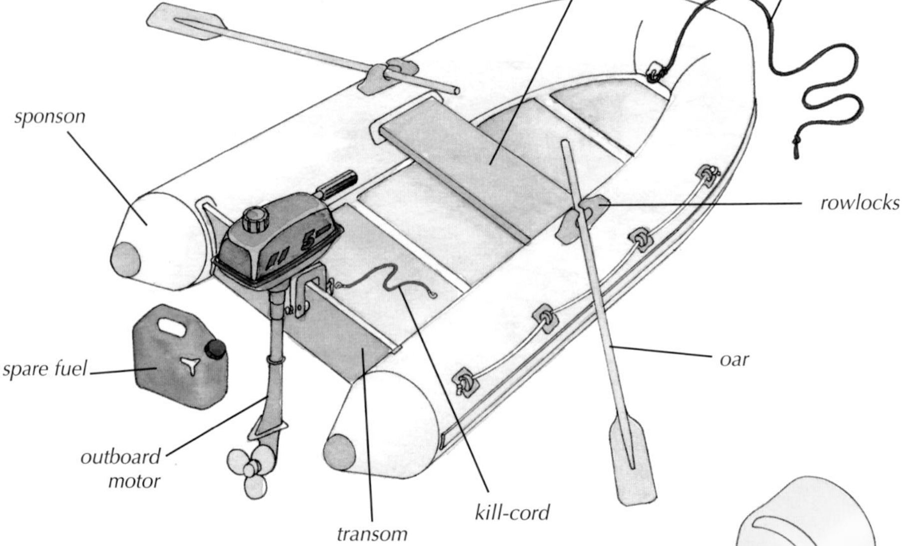

thwart

painter

sponson

rowlocks

spare fuel

oar

outboard motor

kill-cord

transom

Have an anchor onboard.

Carry a box containing:
- tools
- bailer
- flares
- torch
- spark plug
- hand-held VHF

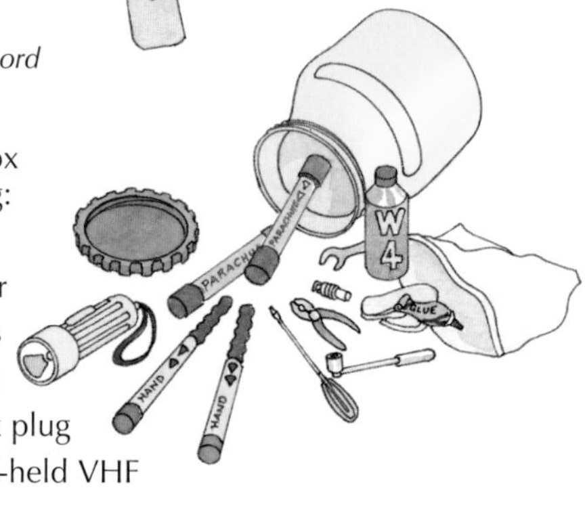

Load the dinghy evenly.

Wear lifejackets and do not overload the boat.

Climb in and out with care.

Ship the oars and glide alongside.

If rowing in a strong tidal stream 'crab' across by heading the bow up into the flow.

tide

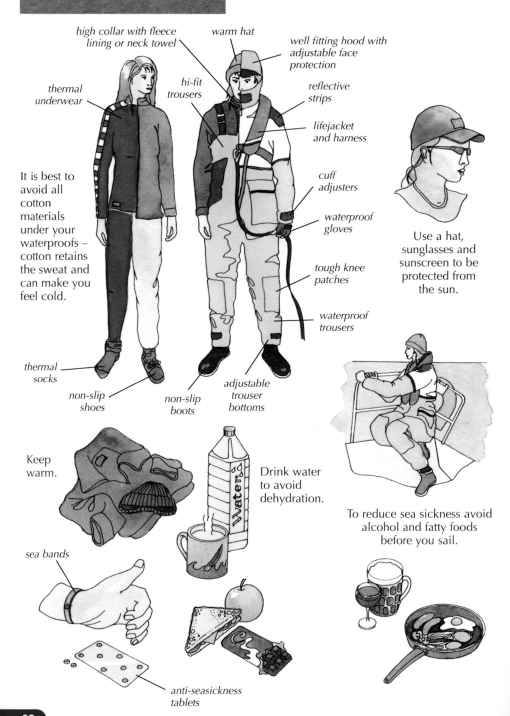

high collar with fleece lining or neck towel

warm hat

well fitting hood with adjustable face protection

thermal underwear

hi-fit trousers

reflective strips

lifejacket and harness

It is best to avoid all cotton materials under your waterproofs – cotton retains the sweat and can make you feel cold.

cuff adjusters

waterproof gloves

tough knee patches

waterproof trousers

Use a hat, sunglasses and sunscreen to be protected from the sun.

thermal socks

non-slip shoes

non-slip boots

adjustable trouser bottoms

Keep warm.

Drink water to avoid dehydration.

To reduce sea sickness avoid alcohol and fatty foods before you sail.

sea bands

anti-seasickness tablets

Lifejackets

A modern gas-inflated lifejacket combined with a harness can be auto-inflating.

Use the crutch straps.

A lifejacket with integral buoyancy will give support to a conscious casualty who is able to swim.

Extra buoyancy can be added by blowing into the valve.

DoT lifejackets found in ships and ferries can be bulky and uncomfortable to wear.

Children need special jackets to fit them.

Lifejackets that are too big or too loose do not provide support in the water and are dangerous. Use crutch straps to keep the jacket down.

Harnesses

Adjust a harness to fit you properly. It must fit tightly to be effective.

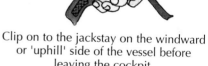

Clip on to the jackstay on the windward or 'uphill' side of the vessel before leaving the cockpit.

Clip onto:
• Jackstays
• D rings
• Shrouds and stays

Don't clip onto:
• Ropes
• Guardrails or anything else

1 Shout "man overboard"
  Point at the casualty in the water.

2 Throw a life-belt and danbuoy.

3 Don't take your eyes off them and keep
  pointing.

The skipper will ask for the
jib to be lowered and start
the engine.

Keep pointing

4 Prepare a throwing line.

5 The skipper will come alongside, boat
  pointing into the wind, propeller stopped.
  Get a line around the casualty. Bring them
  aboard via the stern or boarding ladder - or
  use the halyard and winch them on board.

Common causes of fire

Smoking below decks

Solvents/paints stored below

 Gas build-up in the bilges

 Faulty wiring

Extinguishers

Dry powder – don't use on flammable liquids.
CO_2 – good for enclosed spaces.
AFFF - foam, good for flammable liquids.

 Cooking fats

Fighting the fire

Aim the extinguisher at the base of the flames.

Fire blanket – good for smothering flames.

Splashing water from a bucket can be more effective than throwing its entire contents at once.

Fire blankets can be used to smother a galley fire...

...and they are also essential for clothing fires.

MAYDAY

Only make a Mayday call if there is 'grave and imminent danger' to person or vessel.

Use
- Channel 16
- High power

  Press button on microphone before speaking – release it after the word "over".

VHF/DSC ALERT

Press the emergency button for five seconds to send an undesignated distress alert.

MAYDAY CALL

"MAYDAY, MAYDAY, MAYDAY
This is yacht *Puffin (repeat* x 3)
MAYDAY yacht *Puffin* (MMSI and call sign)"

MAYDAY MESSAGE

"MAYDAY yacht *Puffin* (MMSI and call sign)
In position (give latitude and longitude from GPS)
Nature of distress
Require immediate assistance …. persons on board
Other VITAL information (abandoning to liferaft/have no liferaft) OVER"

Buoyant Orange Smoke

- Daylight use only
- Use within 3 miles of rescuer
- Throw downwind

Cloud lasts 3 or 4 minutes.

wind

Orange hand-held smoke

Cloud lasts about 1 minute.

wind

Orange smoke is easy for rescue helicopter to see.

Hold by the handle only – the metal casing gets very hot.

Red hand-held flare

wind

- Use day or night
- Within 3 miles of rescuer

Hold the flare downwind and horizontally to protect your hands.

Red parachute rocket

Remove cap

10° downwind

Do not use if a rescue helicopter is nearby.

wind

Let off 2 rockets so the observer can take a bearing.

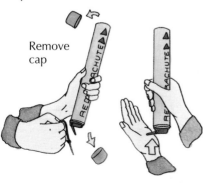

Read the instructions on flares and check they are in date.

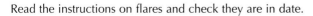

The liferaft should be stowed in a GRP canister on deck. Do not use it as a seat! With an HRU (hydrostatic release unit) it will deploy automatically if the boat sinks.

Only use the liferaft if there is no hope of saving the yacht. If possible stay with the yacht.

Stow a valise liferaft in a locker. Do not put other gear on top of it.

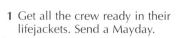

1 Get all the crew ready in their lifejackets. Send a Mayday.

2 Check the painter is tied on.

4 Pull on the painter to inflate the liferaft.

3 Launch the liferaft on the leeward side.

6 Get the crew to climb in, staying dry, if possible. Do not jump into the water.

5 Get a heavy adult into the liferaft first for stability.

7 Take extra things if you can – water, carbohydrate foods, first aid kit, warm clothes, sleeping bags, TPA (thermal protection aid).

8 Cut the painter and stream the drogue to increase the stability and reduce drift. Bail out any water. Take anti-seasickness tablets!

This is more suitable for a cruise liner than a cruising yacht.

Think carefully about the gear that you will need and pack it in a soft waterproof bag.

Turn off taps to save water.

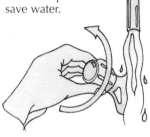

Switch off lights to save power and not to dazzle crew on deck at night.

Clean up!

Turn off after use.

Don't leave the gas while it is lit.

Turn off at the tap away from the cooker.

Turn off at the bottle.

There are many different types of marine lavatory (heads); the one shown below is fairly common. The skipper will usually show the crew how the heads work when you come aboard - if not, it's best to ask.

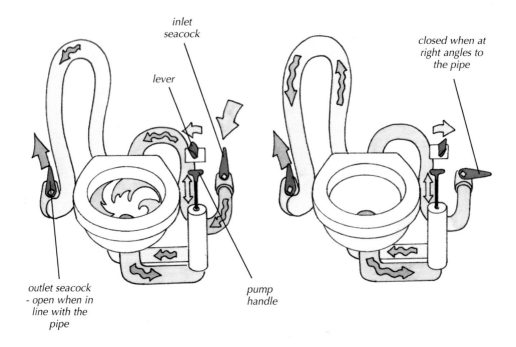

inlet seacock

lever

closed when at right angles to the pipe

outlet seacock - open when in line with the pipe

pump handle

1 To flush, open both seacocks - inlet and outlet.
2 Move the small lever on the pump to the left and pump with the handle about 10 times to discharge the contents into the sea or holding tank.
3 Move the lever to the right and pump the bowl dry.
4 Close both seacocks.

Marine toilets rarely get blocked, if you follow the instructions.

However these are some things that will almost certainly block them.

Do not flush them.

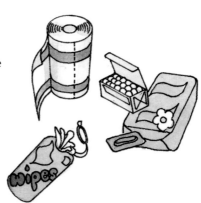

Golden Rules At Sea

- Stow all gear securely
- Shut all lockers and hatches
- Put one chart only on the chart table with no drinks or wet gear

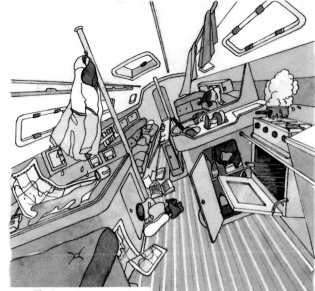

- Clean up spills in the galley immediately
- Put things away in the right place
- Don't waste water or power
- Don't disturb resting crew

Shipping Forecast Areas

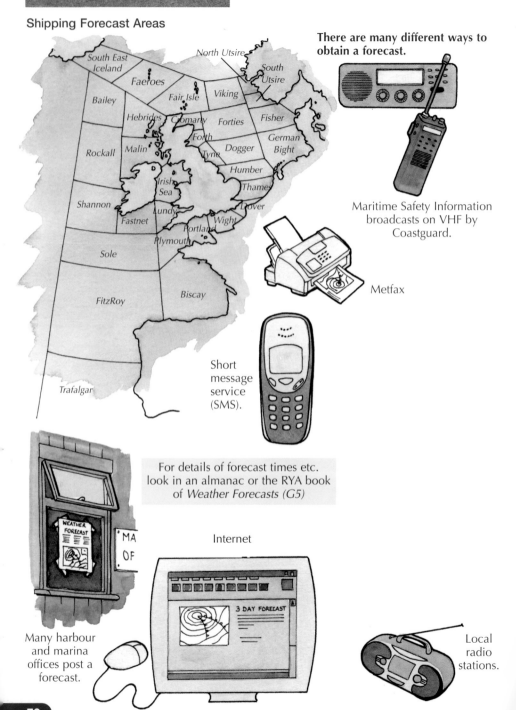

There are many different ways to obtain a forecast.

Maritime Safety Information broadcasts on VHF by Coastguard.

Metfax

Short message service (SMS).

For details of forecast times etc. look in an almanac or the RYA book of *Weather Forecasts (G5)*

Internet

Many harbour and marina offices post a forecast.

Local radio stations.

1 **Light airs** 1 - 3 knots
Ripples.
Sail - drifting conditions

2 **Light breeze** 4 - 6 knots
Small wavelets.
Sail - full mainsail and large genoa

3 **Gentle breeze** 7 - 10 knots
Occasional crests.
Sail - full sail

4 **Moderate** 11 - 16 knots
Frequent white horses.
Sail - reduce headsail size

5 **Fresh breeze** 17 - 21 knots
Moderate waves, many white crests.
Sail - reef mainsail

6 **Strong breeze** 22 - 27 knots
Large waves, white foam crests.
Sail - reef main and reduce headsail

7 **Near gale** 28 - 33 knots
Sea heaps up, spray, breaking waves, foam
blows in streaks.
Sail - deep reefed main, small jib

8 **Gale** 34 - 40 knots
Moderately high waves, breaking crests.
Sail - deep reefed main, storm jib

9 **Severe gale** 41 - 47 knots
High waves, spray affects visibility.
Sail - trysail and storm jib

10 **Storm** 48 - 55 knots
Very high waves, long breaking crests.
Survival conditions

Where do I go from here?

SAIL	SHOREBASED SAIL & MOTOR	MOTOR

Start Yachting
Practical

Essential Navigation & Seamanship

Competent Crew
Practical

Day Skipper
Shorebased

Helmsman's
Practical

Day Skipper
Practical

Coastal Skipper & Yachtmaster
Shorebased

Day Skipper
Practical

Coastal Skipper
Practical

Coastal Skipper
Practical

Yachtmaster Coastal
Certificate of Competence

Yachtmaster Coastal
Certificate of Competence

Yachtmaster Offshore
Certificate of Competence

Yachtmaster Offshore
Certificate of Competence

Yachtmaster Ocean
Shorebased

Yachtmaster Ocean
Certificate of Competence

Yachtmaster Ocean
Oral Exam

Yachtmaster Ocean
Certificate of Competence

RYA One-day Support Course:

Diesel Engine	VHF Radio	Radar	First Aid	Sea Survival

Index

RYA *Membership*

Promoting and Protecting Boating
www.rya.org.uk

Promoting and Protecting Boating

The RYA is the national organisation which represents the interests of everyone who goes boating for pleasure. The greater the membership, the louder our voice when it comes to protecting members' interests. Apply for membership today, and support the RYA, to help the RYA support you.

Benefits of Membership

- Special members' discounts on a range of products and services including boat insurance, books, charts, DVDs and class certificates
- Access to expert advice on all aspects of boating from legal wrangles to training matters
- Free issue of Certificate of Competence; increasingly asked for by overseas governments, holiday companies, insurance underwriters and boat hire companies

- Third Party insurance for windsurfing members
- Access to the wide range of RYA publications, including the RYA quarterly magazine
- E-newsletters, tailored to the type of boating you enjoy, to keep you up to date and give you the chance to join the debate on issues that affect you
- Regular offers in RYA Magazine
- ...and much more

JOIN NOW
Membership form opposite or join online at www.rya.org.uk
Visit our website for information, advice, members' services and web shop.